The Tutor's Handbook
READING
Grade 2

Written by Sally Cardoza Griffith

Illustrated by George Ulrich

Project Manager: Ellen Winkler
Editor: Deborah Ross Klingsporn
Book Design: Rita Hudson
Cover Art Direction and Design: Rita Hudson and Riley Wilkinson
Cover Photos: Anthony Nex Photography
Graphic Artist: Carol Arriola

FS122121 The Tutor's Handbook: Reading Grade 2
All rights reserved—Printed in the U.S.A.
Copyright © 2001 Frank Schaffer Publications, Inc.
23740 Hawthorne Blvd., Torrance, CA 90505

TABLE OF CONTENTS

TUTORS AS COACHES

What Is a Coach?

A coach is someone who encourages, inspires, and educates us to work hard so that we can be our best at something we want to do. A coach envisions what our best looks like and helps us get from where we are to where we want to be. A coach must have a plan of action—a goal and what steps to take to achieve that goal. A coach must tell us how we are progressing and what we need to practice in order to improve. A coach cheers us on from the sidelines, supports us when we falter, and gives us a high five when we succeed.

A child who is struggling in second grade needs a coach—a tutor. A child who is reading below grade level or is working hard to maintain grade level would benefit greatly from one-on-one coaching, or tutoring, from a person who is willing to be like a rock for that child—strong, steady, dependable, and knowledgeable. Are you that person? If you picked up this book, you undoubtedly are! You are interested in helping children and want to be the best you can be as a tutor. So, let this book be your coach as you begin helping a child to be a better reader.

Your goal as a tutor is to help a child become an independent, lifelong reader. This is a big goal—a tremendous goal. This is the most important goal teachers have in the education profession. If a child can't read with comprehension, he or she is in danger of falling behind in the sequential steps of education. A second grader who is struggling with reading needs help immediately. Fourth grade is just around the corner, where the content students are expected to acquire increases considerably. Acquiring knowledge depends on the ability to access information by reading. There is no time to lose. Second grade is an important year for young students.

This book will guide you in developing a plan of action for helping a child improve in reading. With strategies and activities to develop his or her fluency and comprehension, you can foster a love of reading in your second-grade student. The book also promotes the use of writing to help with reading comprehension. All of these abilities will help your student excel in school. This book will also provide you with tools for evaluating the child's progress and will offer suggestions on just what to say to a child, whether he or she is discouraged or encouraged. Are you ready? You can do it! Get your hand ready for some high fives, because the coaching is about to begin!

Get to Know Your Student

The first step in the tutoring process is to get to know your student. There are two reasons to form a comfortable bond with your student. The first is that the relationship between you and your student is unique. It's a one-on-one relationship where you work together very closely. You want your child to feel comfortable with you, comfortable enough to make mistakes, ask questions, be himself or herself. You also want your student to enjoy the tutoring sessions, look forward to them, have some laughs, and feel that learning can be fun. This can all be accomplished in the friendly way you interact with each other. And as you get to know your student, with some of the material below to help, let your student get to know you too, by sharing some of your own stories and interests.

Your student is unique!

The second reason to get to know your student well is so that you can find reading material that will interest him or her. Books and other material that personally appeal to your student will give him or her an added reason to excel—the reading will be great fun.

Below are some qualities that second graders possess. Let this list help you understand the level and capabilities of your student, but don't hesitate to find some additional delightful qualities that are unique to your student.

What Are Second Graders Like?

- They are sincere. They express honest opinions without hesitation.

- They are creative. Their ability to imagine stories and invent games is unlimited.

- They are curious about the world around them

and take pleasure in the thrill of discovery.

- They are generous. They will share their friendship, thoughts, and feelings with people of all ages.

- They are full of life. They have an immeasurable capacity to learn and love.

- They are playful. Join them in a game and share in their laughter.

- They are sensitive. Their feelings can be easily hurt, and they can recognize the feelings of others.

- They are open to learning. They feel exhilarated when they learn something new.

- They are happy that you are helping them and will make your experience very rewarding!

The *Interest Inventory* reproducible on page 11 can help you get to know your student further. Depending on your student's writing ability, you may have to help him or her write the answers to the questions. Asking specific questions like the ones provided will help generate conversations that assist you in choosing books for your student. Find out if he or she would enjoy biographies, mysteries, humorous books, stories about the trials and tribulations of little siblings, *Amelia Bedelia* stories (Margaret Parish, Harper Trophy, 1963) about people who do wacky things, or stories of best friends and crazy teachers. Does your student like pictures of horses, enjoy the seashore, like poetry, want to be an astronaut or a farmer? Whatever his or her interests, there are books on those topics to enjoy!

Your Student's Family

In some cases the struggling reader is a child whose parents have not fostered good reading habits in their home. Perhaps the parents never read aloud to their kids, or were illiterate. Or possibly there is not enough money for books, or the library was an unknown entity. Or it could be that the parents are too busy or too tired to read, or the television dominates the family's leisure time. As a tutor, you should be sensitive to the student and his or her family background.

Communicating with the child's parents or guardians will be an important factor in your success. To begin with, you will want to know what goals or concerns the parents have and how they compare to the child's. If you are planning on giving a child activities to do at home, make sure the parents have the time, materials, or skills needed to assist their child. Be aware of and sensitive to the differences among families. Try to find books that reflect your child's culture (as well as gender) and ones that reflect diverse cultures. Some cultures have storytelling traditions as a way to share stories, rather than writing them. Your student may be able to share some family stories with you. Some questions to consider:

- Does the family speak English as its primary language at home?

- Are there languages in addition to English that the child or family speaks?

- Can the parents read and write English?

- Do the parents and child have time available to work together on homework activities?

- Are there cultural differences that you need to be aware of that will affect how you and the child work together or how you and the parents work together? How does the family observe birthdays? Holidays?

As your tutoring sessions progress, be sure to communicate to parents what you are doing, either through conversations or written notes or both.

The Importance of the Library

The library is a great resource for you and your student. Remember how cool it was to get your very first library card? Take your student to the neighborhood library and get him or her a library card. The child's parents will have to sign the application form because they will be the ones responsible for lost books. Some struggling readers have families who are not familiar with the library. If this is the case, consider yourself a tour guide and invite the whole family on a field trip. Show the family the sections on books written in their language if English is not their first language, take them to the children's section and the adult section, and show them how to check out books. Knowing where and how to get books that are free of charge is a major step to becoming a lifelong reader. And having Mom and Dad accompany the student to the library provides great motivation.

A child who is learning to read needs a steady supply of books all the time. You can probably get

some from the child's teacher, but don't depend on this. The teacher needs to be rotating the books he or she has throughout the class. Don't assume that you or the parents can buy all the books you will need; this would be too costly, and some books that you choose might end up being too easy or too hard. If they are from the library, you can just put them in the return slot if they aren't at the appropriate level. But if you bought them, then you'll feel committed to them. The library is the key here; by using it, you can keep a

student in a steady supply of books, and most important, you'll be modeling how to use the library. You might even do your tutoring at the library—as long as the librarian will allow you to read aloud.

The librarian can direct you to books at the appropriate level for your student. You might want to explore the library's computerized catalog also. Your student can type in a favorite subject, such as *cats* or *bicycles*, and get a list of titles. There are also periodicals suitable for second graders at most libraries.

What You Need to Begin Tutoring

When in a tutoring session, you and your student must be comfortable. The setting you work in should help you both be comfortable and enable you to concentrate. You need a place that is quiet—with no television, no siblings interrupting you, and no friends knocking on the door wondering when you'll be finished so "Johnny" or "Jenny" can go out to play. Can you work in the local library? Perhaps you can find an empty classroom at the child's school, a quiet kitchen table, or maybe a corner of a living room. The *Door Hanger and Nameplate* reproducible on page 12 can be photocopied on heavy paper and colored by your student. Use the door hanger and nameplate as a way to establish a quiet setting for tutoring sessions or homework time.

You will need a desk or table, a lamp or light bright enough to read comfortably by, paper, scissors, pencils, crayons, and a stapler. Wherever you are, be sure you can have this setting week after week, so that you and your student become assured of your place and committed to the routine of going there to learn. If you think that your student will not be too distracted by the surroundings, you can try working outdoors.

When moms and dads read to their children, it's usually a snuggly experience with lots of affection. When you read to your student, you cannot imitate that experience for a couple of reasons. One—it is not appropriate to become that physically close with your student. Two—you cannot replace the parents, even if you are committed to helping the child read. The experience will be different than that which the parents can give the child; it will still be valuable, however. You can sit shoulder to shoulder with the child; you can pat his or her hand or shake it. A good relationship with your student can be developed with some of the methods of praise listed below.

Ways to Encourage Your Student

A child needs to receive positive feedback. He or she may not get individual attention in school, where he or she is but one of dozens in a classroom. As a tutor, you can make your student feel valued for his or her efforts and accomplishments. Children thrive under these conditions. Think how great you feel when someone gives you a thumbs up for work you've done. Praise the behavior that you want to encourage. Here are some different ways to say "Good job!" to your student so that he or she will know that you really mean it.

Examples:

"Leslie, I noticed that you reread that phrase when you didn't understand it. That's what good readers do!"

"Ben, you have all of your supplies ready to use. You are really well prepared today."

"Maria, I'm enjoying reading aloud to you so much because you are listening very carefully. Thank you!"

By noticing improvement or positive effort, you are encouraging a child to strive to be even better the next time. The child will want to continue to do well. Sometimes, though, a child gets discouraged and requires finesse in handling. Learning to read is hard work, and the child may feel tired and defeated at times. Be empathetic and encouraging to your student during these times. Realize that when you start to feel frustration, your student probably does too, so you know just how he or she feels. Below are some methods for dealing with a frustrated student.

Examples:

"Reading is hard work, isn't it, Leslie? You're having trouble decoding this word. I'll bet you remember the strategy we used yesterday for the word *invisible*. Right! You remembered that we found a little word in the big word. What little word can you find in this word? Aha! That's just what good readers do. Let's try the next sentence."

"Ben, I know sometimes it's hard to think about what to write next in a story. Sometimes it just makes you want to throw your pencil out the window! I have an idea. Let's think of the craziest thing in the world that could happen next in your story. If it's a good idea, you can use it. If not, we'll think again." (By getting a child to laugh, you lower the frustration level. Ben may not use the crazy idea, but his creative juices will start flowing. Help him with another idea or two; then leave him to continue independently.)

"Maria, that sentence is a doozy! I can understand why you are having a bit of trouble with it. Tell me what good readers do when they are stuck. Now, my good reader, what will you do?"

Be sure to make reading fun!

Rewards

Verbally praising a child for his or her good efforts as soon as you see a desired behavior is an effective way to encourage him or her to repeat the behavior. Praise from you is indeed a wonderful motivator. Sometimes, though, a child simply needs a treat—a sticker, a colorful pencil, an interesting eraser, a pad of sticky notes. These are things that second-grade girls and boys love. Don't give treats routinely. Think like a magician, and every now and then pull a reward "out of your hat" for a job well done. Also, remember your student's birthday. When it's your student's special day, stick a happy birthday sticker on his or her shirt, give him a birthday pencil or a little cupcake, and you will have a student who feels appreciated. The *Bookmarks* reproducible on page 13 can be photocopied on heavy paper, cut, and colored by your student. Use the bookmarks as rewards or as an activity when your student is having difficulty being still. The award certificate reproducible on page 14 is another way to reward a hardworking student.

Discipline

A tutor who is working one on one with a student and using lots of praise shouldn't encounter discipline problems. However, when you have a student who is distracted, unfocused, or unwilling to work, you need to talk to him or her. Ask the child why he or she isn't trying. Listen to the response. The student may be tired, worried, hungry, nervous about problems at home, angry at a sibling—the list is endless. If the problem is serious, discuss it with the parents and teacher. Your student may be in a power struggle with you, as in "I'm not going to work and you can't make me." It's true—you can't really make a child work. At times like this it is important not to give up; you need to model perseverance and a commitment to your student. Let him or her know that you will still be there even when the student's behavior isn't perfect. If the student doesn't or can't concentrate on doing the work, then read aloud to him or her.

> **Be a model of perseverance and commitment to your student.**

You can try switching to another activity if your student is frustrated, unmotivated, or uncooperative. Switch to writing, have the child draw a picture of something you're reading together, or play with flash cards. Whatever you do, don't go away. Don't let the student win by making you angry or making you think helping him or her is hopeless. This child is at risk, and you, as a tutor, have great potential in recovering the child's reading ability. Stay put. You will win the child's respect, and he or she will be relieved to learn that this adult is not going to let him or her down.

Attitude

Some children have an I-can't-do-it attitude. Usually they can do it, but they want attention from you. First, you must decide if the work is at the proper level for your student's ability. Is the student genuinely attempting the task but looking dazed and confused? If so, the work is probably too difficult. Either help the child through it or give him or her something else to do.

The attention-seeking child will quickly glance at a task and give up before he or she tries. With this child, you need to be simple and direct: "I know you can do it. I'm going to set this timer and give you ten minutes to finish this job. Can you beat the clock? Go!" Urge this child to work independently. Then invite the student to say "I can do it!"

> **Encourage the student to take risks.**

Children need to be reassured that they are capable of learning to read. Sometimes a task needs to be broken into smaller parts so that a child can successfully complete it. This strategy is important for developing a positive attitude. Children also need to know why learning is important. A struggling reader must realize that learning to read well will help him or her throughout life. How does a child realize this? Bring in your electric bill, a cereal box, insurance papers, a check book, a menu. Show the student all of the different kinds of things that adults must read. Talk about the consequences of not knowing how to read, such as not knowing what to order at a restaurant or having the electricity turned off because you didn't know where to send the check.

It's Okay to Make Mistakes

It *is* okay to make mistakes, and this is an important concept for a struggling reader. Teaching a child that mistakes are okay gives him or her permission to take a risk. The student will feel free to try to blend a word or attempt to give an opinion about the meaning of a story. If the child makes a mistake, he or she will probably try again. If he or she looks at you for confirmation, you can simply say "Think again" or "Does that make sense?" rather than "No, you're wrong." Let the student know you trust him or her to discover the answer. Don't supply an answer after one wrong one from the student. Your job is to guide him or her down the correct road. If, after a while, the child doesn't get the answer, say "How about this?" and give it to him or her. Let the student affirm it. By assisting him or her in this reaffirming way, you will help the child develop a confident attitude.

Responsibility

One way a student is asked to be responsible is by completing homework assignments. A child who struggles in school could have poor homework habits. Successfully completing and returning homework develops responsibility in a child. It helps to tell a child that just as exercising makes our arms and legs and heart strong, studying makes our brain strong. A tutoring session can be a time for a student to complete an assignment or have you go over the work with him or her. Many students have trouble remembering their assignments or materials needed to do the homework. As a coach, you can emphasize the following points to help a child establish good homework habits.

- **Structure** For example, do reading first, math second; finish one assignment before going on to the next. Work in an environment that is not distracting.

- **Organization** Does the student have all books, papers, supplies necessary and at hand? Does the student understand the assignment and have it in writing if necessary?

- **Routine** What is the best time each day for this particular child to do homework? Does he or she need a snack before getting down to work?

Children work in different ways because people learn in different ways. Some children must have silence in order to work. Some must have the radio on in order to concentrate. Some students need short breaks between tasks. Some need to plow through without stopping until finished. What is important is to figure out what works for your student, and then to help him or her make this homework style a habit. Mom and Dad might be asked to help by making sure the child has a homework spot and a place to put his or her finished homework. Often children put their homework in their backpacks and leave them by the front door, ready to grab on their way out. If a child is having a problem with homework, figure out where the breakdown occurs. Some simply forget to bring their assignments home, and some forget to take them back to school. There are lots of potholes on the road to good homework habits, and a good tutor helps pave the road. Remember, the teacher and the parents are there to support your efforts. Elicit their help in helping the child.

Part of being a responsible student is being aware of time and using it wisely. Some second graders are still struggling with how to tell time. Use the reproducible on page 15, *What Time Is It?* to help your student with this skill.

Interest Inventory

1 Do you have any brothers or sisters? How old are they? What are they like?

_____

_____

2 What do you enjoy doing with your family?

_____

_____

3 Who are your friends? Why do you like them? What do you do together?

_____

_____

4 What sports or games do you like to play?

_____

_____

5 What are your favorite books? Favorite TV programs? Favorite movies?

_____

_____

6 Do you have any pets? If not, what animals do you like?

_____

_____

7 What are three things you like about school?

_____

_____

Are there things you don't like about school?

_____

8 How can I help you?

_____

_____

Use the back of this page to draw a picture of yourself having fun.

Door Hanger and Nameplate

My Homework Place

DO NOT DISTURB
great mind at work

Directions: Color and cut with scissors. Use when studying or during a tutoring session.

12
reproducible

Bookmarks

Reward your student with these fun and motivating bookmarks. Photocopy them on cardstock and let the child color them.

I am learning to read and write.

I like reading books!

I am a good reader!

13
reproducible

With great admiration,

this certificate is awarded to

_____

for hard work and great effort

in reading and writing.

Congratulations on your achievement.

_____   _____
        Tutor   Date

What Time Is It?

Draw the hands on the watch for each time shown.

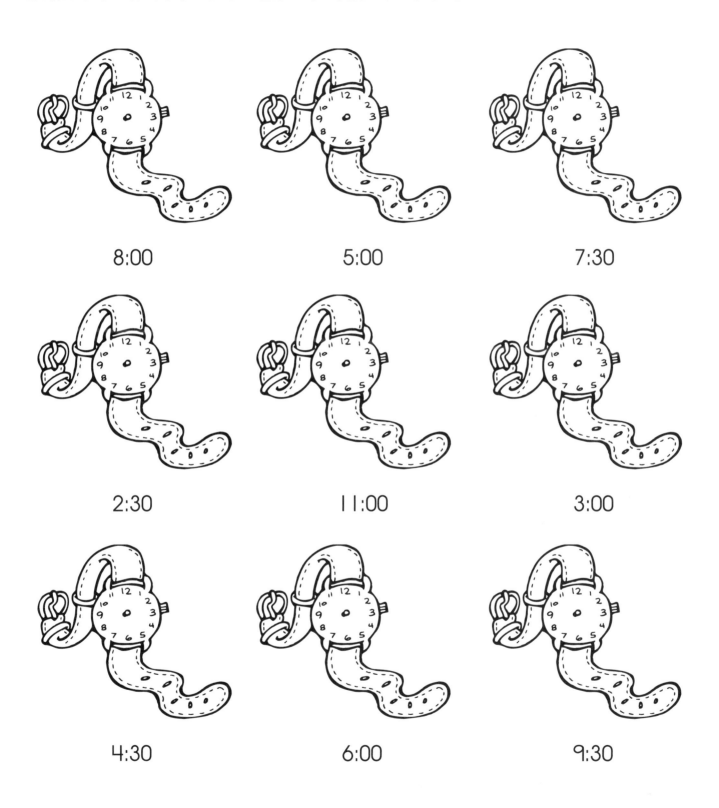

8:00   5:00   7:30

2:30   11:00   3:00

4:30   6:00   9:30

EVALUATING YOUR STUDENT'S READING ABILITY AND PROGRESS

What Do Good Readers Do?

It is important when evaluating a student's reading ability to understand exactly what it is that good readers do when they come upon a word that they don't know. Think about it for a minute. What do you do if you're reading a recipe that is very unfamiliar, very exact in its directions? Or what if you're reading a book for an advanced science class or any text that is difficult? Usually, a good reader will slow down, break the hard word apart, and then blend it together. He or she might reread the entire sentence. Another tactic would be to read ahead for context clues and then return to read the sentence again. Often the reader will pronounce the word or mouth it silently as he or she figures it out. Sometimes a good reader will just read on, realizing that not being able to pronounce the word or understand its meaning does not take away from his or her comprehension of the passage. In order to tutor reading, you need to know what behaviors to look for that promote good reading. What do good readers do?

> **Encourage your student to make an "educated guess" when stuck on a word. Mistakes are okay!**

Good readers . . .

- read for meaning; they want to make sense of the text

- read with fluency

- use expression when reading aloud

- understand punctuation, such as pausing at commas

- reread

- know when to skip a difficult word

- sometimes pause to think about what they're reading

- use illustrations to help understand the text

- use reading strategies for difficult words or passages

- enjoy reading

As you work with your student, teach him or her more of the strategies of a good reader. (See page 39.) These strategies become the child's keys to unlocking the treasure of a book.

The cuing systems are as follows:

1. **Graphophonics:** the written sounds of our oral language. This includes letter recognition, letter-sound relationships, spelling patterns, and unpredictable letter-sound relationships.

2. **Semantics:** the meaning that the words convey.

3. **Syntax:** the structure of language. This is the proper order of words that a language uses.

When you listen to a child read, and watch him or her try to problem-solve when he or she gets stuck, you can (with practice) realize in which cuing system extra help is needed. If the student consistently has difficulty decoding words, then he or she needs more phonics activities. However, if the child is only depending on decoding words to read, without comprehending, then he or she needs to understand that there are two more cuing systems. Is he or she using what has happened thus far in the story to predict what a word might be? Is the child using what he or she knows about the English language to determine that the sentence *Mary wore a dress red* isn't correct? A child must learn to process these systems through the computer that is his or her brain. The student must constantly be thinking, monitoring his or her progress, correcting errors by rereading, rethinking, reblending, and so on.

The Reading Process

One of the first tasks to perform as a tutor will be to determine exactly what a child is having difficulty with in reading. To assess your student, you will need to observe and record his or her behavior.

The reading process is made up of three parts, called *cuing systems.* Each of these parts is equal in weight to the others, and no part can be ignored.

Don't forget to record each session to track your student's progress.

Running Records

There are a number of ways to monitor a student's reading progress. One way is a *running record*. A running record is used to check the accuracy of a child's oral reading. It is used to determine what cuing system the child relies upon the most, and which one or ones he or she neglects. In a running record, a child reads a passage of about 100 words. The tutor has a copy of the passage. The tutor places a check mark over each word the child reads correctly. The tutor writes any incorrect words that the child says over the actual word in the text. If the child rereads any part of the text, the tutor draws an arrow over that part to show it was reread and writes the symbol *RR* next to the arrow. If the child self-corrects a word, the tutor writes *SC* next to that word. In this way, a tutor can determine how many errors a child makes in a particular passage (self-corrections are not counted as errors). Take the total number of words and divide it by the number of errors. This determines the error ratio. A ratio of 1:10 or higher (for example, 1:17) means the student made 1 error for every 10 words read. This ratio indicates that the text is a good one for the child to read in order to work on his or her reading strategies. If the error ratio is 1:9 or below, the text is too difficult for the child; he or she will tend to lose the text's meaning.

One ✓ ✓ ✓ ✓
Once/upon a time/there
SC RR
saw/ ✓ ✓ dinosaur
was/an evil dragon
SC
✓ live-ed ✓ ✓ ✓
that lived in a cave.

The Five Finger Rule

You will want to get books at the proper level for your student, ones that allow him or her to work on the particular reading strategies that need attention. You can do running records on passages of books to see if they are at the child's level, or you can use the Five Finger Rule. This is by no means as informative as a running record, but it is still a handy tool. It is easy enough for the student to use when picking out his or her own books. The Five Finger Rule is simply this: When reading one typical page from a book, the child puts up a finger for each word he or she can't read. If he or she uses all five fingers before finishing the page, that book is probably too difficult. The child should choose an easier book.

Remember to praise your student's hard work.

Use the Teacher and the Parents As Sources of Information

In order to gather more information about your student's reading level, talk to his or her teacher. Ask the teacher to give you his or her expert opinions and advice. Request that the teacher show you the child's test scores, writing samples, journals, and spelling work. If the teacher uses running records, ask him or her to show them to you. Also, find out about your student's homework habits, social skills, and so on. The *Teacher Input Form* reproducible on page 22 can help you when speaking with the teacher. Talk to the child's parents as well. Ask what the parents see as their child's problem and what specific goals they expect the child to achieve. Considering all aspects of the child will help you to understand and to know the person, and thus, to help him or her.

Anecdotal Notes and Portfolios

Anecdotal notes are among the most useful tools you can use as a tutor to monitor progress. An anecdotal note is simply what you observe your student doing. An easy way to keep these notes is to write them in a journal. For every session with your child, use a page in the journal. Date it at the top.

Examples of anecdotal notes:

- When you see your student finally remembering to pause at commas, write it down: *Ben remembered to pause at commas for the first time.*

- When you see your student thumbing through a book, looking at pictures, and briefly scanning the text, write it down: *Ben was searching for meaning even before he started to read.*

- If your student is neglecting a strategy, write it down: *Ben neglects the silent* e *endings in words. He's still using a short vowel sound in words such as* made.

As you review your journal, you will discover what you need to teach. Now that Ben is remembering commas, how is he doing with exclamation points? Now that Ben is searching for meaning even before he begins to read, it's time for him to verbalize predictions and check for their accuracy. Ben still needs work with long *a* spellings. Time to pull out the magnetic letters and build words with short vowels, then add the silent *e*.

Your journal will also serve as a record of your time with your student. It's a handy place to store information that you will use to evaluate your student, so that you may show Mom and Dad the strides that the child is making, and the areas in which he or she is still struggling. The *Tutoring Session Log* reproducible on page 23 is another way you can record the progress and areas that need work after each session.

An additional way to record your student's efforts is to keep a portfolio of his or her work. A portfolio is simply a folder in which you collect running records, writing samples, loose-leaf anecdotal notes, completed reproducible pages, and other things that show you something about the child's progress. Over time, as you look through the portfolio, you and the student will be able to see steady growth as you compare earlier samples of work to later ones.

> **Tell your student how reading has enriched your life.**

October 16 Reba is searching for meaning by looking at the pictures.

Student Journal

Your student can keep a journal as well. Each time he or she meets with you, the student dates the top of a page. At the end of each session, he or she writes one thing learned—be it a strategy, a new spelling of a long vowel sound, that adjectives go before nouns, that he or she really loves to read nonfiction books about sea life. The student can also write one thing that he or she needs to practice during the week—reading with expression, for example. Writing down what was learned and what needs practice will encourage the student to start thinking about his or her learning and take responsibility for it. The child will begin to feel empowered, in control of his or her reading skills.

Your student can also keep a record of his or her progress with the reproducible *My Reading Log*, on page 24. This form helps the student keep track of all the books he or she has read. Once the chart is filled, praise the student for his or her hard work. This would be a good time to pull a small prize out of your hat!

Have your student take part in assessment. Evaluate the work together and let the student tell you where he or she needs to improve.

Remember, assessment comes in many forms. The most important aspect of assessing is being a good "kid-watcher." Be like a scientist and observe the child, record your findings, use them to guide your teaching, and then evaluate. Always have a pencil in hand and your journal ready.

Assessing Phonetic Skills

Second graders are expected to know the graphophonic system. They need to learn a lot in second grade, and the struggling reader needs lots of practice with the different spelling patterns. Page 25, the *Assessment of Phonetic Skills* reproducible, encompasses words that second graders should know. If you find your student is weak in a certain area of the test, then you will know where you should start your teaching. You and the student should each have a copy of the test. As he or she reads each word in the two columns, check the line next to those that are read correctly. If the student reads any incorrectly, write what he or she says on the line next to the word.

The following page is an overview of the phonetic principles a second grader should know.

About the Assessment of Phonetic Skills

List One of the *Assessment of Phonetic Skills* reproducible on page 25 contains words that have short *a* and long *a* (*ai, a__e, a, ay, eigh*); short *e* and long *e* (*ee, ea, ey, y, e*); diphthongs *oi* and *ou*; *r*-influenced vowels *ir, er*, and *ur*; and /r/ spelled *wr*.

> **Praise your student for being a good listener.**

List Two contains words with short *i* (*i, ui*) and long *i* (*i__e, igh, y*); words with short *o* and long *o* (*o, o__e, oa, ow, oe, ew*); words with short *u* and long *u* (*ue, ew, oo, u__e, ui*); short *oo* words; /f/ spelled *ph*; and a pair of homophones (*so* and *sew*).

These words are examples of what second graders should learn about phonics. In addition they should know the sounds /sh/, /ch/, /th/, /wh/, and /ng/. Second graders should be blending sounds together to make words; for example, "c-r-o-w-n, cr-own, crown." Look to see where your student made errors. Does he or she need practice with long *e* spellings? Or perhaps the student needs extra work with *r*-controlled words such as *work, worse, worm,* and *world*. Is he or she able to read double consonants at the end of a word such as *call*? Second graders also are learning spellings for the sounds /j/ (*j, ge, gi, dge*) and /s/ (*s, ce, ci,*).

Use this assessment as a starting place for your teaching. Consider it another way to observe what your student knows, and what he or she needs to practice. Keep this assessment in the student's portfolio. If your student had great difficulty with it, give it to him or her again after you've been working together for a while.

Many words that children learn must be learned as sight words, because they either defy the phonetic rules that apply to most words or they are used so frequently that children need to learn them as quickly as possible. These are known as high-frequency words, since they are used most often. Some high-frequency or sight words are *the, am,* and *was*. Once a child can read these words automatically, his or her reading will become much smoother and fluency will greatly improve.

A list of high-frequency words is provided for you on the reproducible on page 26, *High-Frequency Words and Second-Grader Words*. Use this list as another way to test your student. A second grader should be able to both read and spell these words. Also included in the list are several words that second graders tend to use often in their writing.

Use the *Flashcards* reproducible on page 27 to help your student become familiar with these commonly misspelled words. Use the backs of the flashcards to write words that your student is having difficulty learning.

CHAPTER 2

Teacher Input Form

Name of child _____ Date _____

1 What is this child's reading level?

    Nonreader   Pre-primer   Primer   First Grade   Above First Grade

2 How well does this child do in the following areas? (Use this key, comments, or both to record answers: E = Excellent   VG = Very Good   G = Good   N = Needs Help)

  a. Oral reading _____

  b. Comprehension _____

  c. Phonics _____

      beginning consonants _____

      short vowels _____

      long vowels _____

      consonant blends _____

  d. Spelling _____

  e. Writing _____

      Writing a story _____

      Capitalization and punctuation _____

      Printing ability _____

  f. Speaking skills _____

  g. Listening skills _____

  h. Work habits _____

3 Is there any other information about this child you think would be helpful to know?

_____

_____

4 What do you think would be the best areas for me to focus on?

_____

_____

5 Do you have any materials you could share with me in those areas?

6 Could I have a copy of the writing paper and handwriting style you use in class?

Tutoring Session Log

Name of child _____ Date _____

A. Tutor Reads Aloud (5–10 minutes)

_____

_____

B. Student Rereads a Book (5 minutes)

_____

_____

C. Working with Words (5-10 minutes)

Phonics _____

_____

Sight Word Vocabulary _____

_____

D. Reading a New Book (10 minutes)

_____

_____

E. Writing Together (10 minutes)

_____

_____

F. Summary/Plan Ahead/Homework (5 minutes)

What went well _____

_____

_____

Next time _____

_____

_____

Homework _____

_____

_____

 **Name** _____

My Reading Log

Titles of the books I've read: Number
                                                                  of pages:

1. _____   _____

2. _____   _____

3. _____   _____

4. _____   _____

5. _____   _____

6. _____   _____

7. _____   _____

8. _____   _____

9. _____   _____

10. _____   _____

I read _____ books!   I read _____ pages!

I AM A SUPER READER!

FS122121 The Tutor's Handbook: Reading Grade 2

Assessment of Phonetic Skills

List One

1. bat _____
2. mail _____
3. lean _____
4. sound _____
5. pray _____
6. foil _____
7. field _____
8. set _____
9. bread _____
10. plane _____
11. tall _____
12. defeat _____
13. be _____
14. gown _____
15. eight _____
16. say _____
17. need _____
18. scar _____
19. wren _____
20. bird _____
21. concert _____
22. joy _____
23. speck _____
24. hurt _____
25. baby _____
26. money _____

List Two

1. lip _____
2. rice _____
3. dot _____
4. cube _____
5. coast _____
6. bright _____
7. know _____
8. clue _____
9. bug _____
10. bolt _____
11. built _____
12. try _____
13. phone _____
14. few _____
15. Joe _____
16. fruit _____
17. could _____
18. hook _____
19. work _____
20. broom _____
21. junk _____
22. lock _____
23. so _____
24. sew _____
25. song _____
26. should _____

Tutor: Put a check mark on the line next to those words the student reads correctly. If the word is read incorrectly, write what the student says on the line.

High-Frequency Words and Second-Grader Words

A: a, about, after, all, am, an, and, any, are, as, asked, at, away

B: back, be, because, been, before, big, boy, but, by

C: came, can, come, could

D: day, did, do, down

E: every, everyone

F: first, for, friend, from

G: get, girl, go, going, got

H: had, has, have, he, her, here, him, his, house, how

I: I, if, I'm, in, into, is, it

J: jump, just

K: keep, kind, know

L: like, little, look

M: made, make, me, mother, more, my

N: no, not, now

O: of, off, old, on, once, one, only, or, our, out, over

P: play, people, put

Q: quiet

R: ran, run

S: said, say, saw, school, see, she, should, so, some

T: that, the, their, them, then, there, they, this, to, too, two

U: up, us

V: very

W: was, we, well, went, were, what, when, where, which, who, will, with, would

Y: you, your

Tutor: Second graders should be able to read and spell these words. Check words that can't be read, and circle words that can't be spelled.

Flashcards

Directions: These are flashcards for some of the most frequently misspelled *w* words. Reproduce them on cardstock. Use the backs to write words that your student is having difficulty learning.

who	what
where	when
why	want
were	went
would	won't

STRATEGIES FOR TEACHING READING

Phonemic Awareness

A *phoneme* is a speech sound. The suffix *eme* refers to a basic unit, or element, of language. *Phon* means "sound" or "voice." A *grapheme* is a letter or letters written to represent a phoneme. *Graph* means "drawn, written, or recorded." For example, in the word *desk* there are four phonemes: /d/, /e/, /s/, and /k/. There are also four graphemes: d, e, s, and k. In the word *she* there are two phonemes: /sh/ and /e/. There are also two graphemes: *sh* and e. However, the word *she* has three letters. The letters *sh* represent one sound—one phoneme—so they cannot be separated.

What gets so tricky for children is that the English alphabet has only 26 letters but has 44 separate phonemes. Not only do different combinations of letters work together to represent distinct sounds—/ch/, /sh/, and /th/, for example—but some sounds can be represented in more than one way. Consider /f/ (the *f* sound) in *graph, fat,* and *tough.* Or the long *e* sound in *eat, speed, lucky, monkey,* and *field.* No wonder students get confused! When learning to read, a child is making the connection between the phonemes of the spoken language and the graphemes of the written language. The child is connecting the sounds that he or she speaks to letters that he or she sees.

> **Compose a poem with your student to develop phonemic awareness.**

Consider, now, the child who does not yet have a good command of the spoken language. Consider the child who still does not have a vast vocabulary to describe his or her world, his or her thoughts, his or her ideas. Consider the child who does not hear the difference between the words *still* and *steal.* Imagine that child trying to read this sentence: *That fat, tough robber is still trying to steal our flat rubber tires.* Granted, this sentence will not win a prize, but can you see where a child who is not facile with his or her oral language will get stuck? Not only does the child need to know graphemes, such as *gh* = /f/, *ou* = short *u*, *ea* = long *e*, *ou* = /ow/, but he or she must have prior knowledge of robbers, rubber tires that are flat, stealing, fat as opposed to thin, tough as opposed to wimpy, and that *still* means "continuing into the present," all in order to make sense of this one sentence. Children have so much work to do when learning to read and must be well prepared. In order to be able to read graphemes, they must first be aware of phonemes. They must have *phonemic awareness.*

Phonemic awareness possibly begins the day Daddy sings "You Are My Sunshine" to Mommy's tummy, but it certainly begins the day baby hears language for the first time, whenever that is! It begins the day Grandma peers over the cradle and says, "Oh, Jeanne, you are such a gorgeous little girl!" It continues as Mommy and Daddy coo and whisper and sing to their baby and talk between themselves.

The baby is hearing the phonemes of his or her language as they are all put together to create words, phrases, sentences, and thus, as they create meaning. When the baby talks, he or she is using what he or she knows of those phonemes to communicate. "Da-da," "ma-ma," and "ba-ba" show the phonemes of which he or she is aware. As the baby grows and learns and listens and practices, he or she will be able to hear many more phonemes—"daddy," "mommy," "bottle"—and be able to use them in his or her speech. The more of those 44 phonemes a child distinguishes and uses, the better prepared he or she is to figure them out when they are written in the code of the alphabet, and the better able he or she is to decode them.

One of your tasks as a tutor is to make sure your student is aware of phonemes. Many children with reading problems still do not hear and attend to all the sounds of the language. They have difficulty distinguishing one sound from a similar sound. Your student must be able to make those distinctions, especially by second grade. Children who are learning English as a second language have a tremendous task. They must learn the sounds of the language, the alphabetic code, the meaning of the words that the combined letters represent, and the structure of the words as they're built into sentences and paragraphs.

One way students become phonemically aware is through word play. Close your eyes (after you read this paragraph, please) and imagine that you are in elementary school. Imagine you are jump-ing rope. What did you jump rope to? Did you jump to one of these rhymes?

"Not last night but the night before
Twenty four robbers came knocking at the door;
As I ran out, they ran in,
And I hit them on the head with a rolling pin!"

"Blue bells, cockle shells, eevy, ivy, over."

"Ice cream soda, Delaware punch;
Spell the initials of your honeybunch—
A, B, C, D, E, F, G, . . ."

Notice the rhyme, the rhythm. Imagine the practice with language that happens when children jump rope to catchy poems like these. This is how phonemic awareness develops even further. As children use and play with language, they learn it. Nursery rhymes, rhyming games, "I see something that starts with an *L*" types of games—these all help to promote awareness of the sounds of language. *Anna Banana: 101 Jump-Rope Rhymes*, by Joanna Cole (Morrow, 1989) has many humorous rhymes your student will love to read and recite.

When you are working with your student and you both need a break, go outside and jump rope to the above rhymes or your own old favorites. If you have a student who does not want to jump rope, dribble a basketball in time to the rhymes or toss a beanbag back and forth as you chant. Phonemic awareness also develops through singing, chanting, and listening to stories and poetry. A variety of oral language activities can help prepare a young reader for graphophonics lessons. The reproducible worksheet found on page 44, *Syllable Stumper,* will give your student further practice in phonemic awareness. *Jaha and Jamil Went Down the Hill: An African Mother Goose* (Virginia Kroll, Charlesbridge, 1995) applies the rhythm of familiar Mother Goose rhymes to verses about African culture and is a good resource for language play.

The next sections will give you specific information on targeting phonemic awareness. The activities focus on the beginning, middle, and ending sounds of words.

Ways to Teach Phonemic Awareness

For teaching these activities you can use a hand puppet who will be your "teaching partner." For example, you might use a wolf puppet named Wally. Wally and you will work together to elicit responses from your student.

Lesson One: Beginning Sound Change

Tutor: I am going to say a word, and Wally is going to say a sound. Your job is to change the beginning sound of the word that I say to the sound that Wally says. For example, if I say *man,* and Wally says /p/, you say *pan.* Here we go. I say *book.*

Wally: /l/

Child: *Look*

Tutor: Great listening. I say *jar.*

Wally: /st/

Child: *Star*

The lesson continues. Here are some words and sounds to use:

bat, /m/	mutton, /b/	breeze, /f/
bank, /th/	dark, /sh/	nice, /d/
glide, /s/	zero, /h/	howl, /y/
mild, /w/	chore, /m/	face, /l/
moo, /z/	merry, /b/	free, /t/

Note how your student does with these beginning changes. If he or she is struggling, obviously more practice is needed. Lesson Two contains more beginning sound work.

Lesson Two: What Sound Did I Drop?

Tutor: I am going to say a word, and then Wally will repeat the word after me, but he will forget to say a sound. Your job is to say the sound that Wally forgets to say. Ready? I say *water*.

Wally: *ater* (with the /aw/ sound at the beginning)

Child: /w/

Tutor: Yes. Wally forgot the /w/ sound. Next one. I say *cheese*.

Wally: *eese*

Child: /ch/

Continue the lesson with the following words without the beginning sounds, having the student say what sounds are dropped.

stroller, roller, /st/   moth, oth, /m/

sweet, weet, /s/   more, ore, /m/

mother, other, /m/   skate, kate, /s/

pizza, izza, /p/   threw, rew, /th/

chicken, icken, /ch/   kitchen, itchen, /k/

library, ibrary, /l/   famous, amous, /f/

Note again how your student does with these beginning sounds. If he or she is continuing to have difficulty, more practice is needed. Make your own lists of words. Use words that hold interest for your particular child. (Think of his or her hobbies.)

Lesson Three: Identify the Ending Sound

Tutor: I am going to say a word. Wally is going to repeat the word, but he will leave off the ending sound. Your job will be to tell me the sound that Wally forgets. Ready? I say *team*.

Wally: *tea*

Child: /m/

If you are sitting next to the child, move your hand from left to right as you slowly say the word, and poke the air at the end—"t e a m"—POKE! Do this a few times until the child gets the feel for the end of the word. Stop using your hand after several times and see if the child can do it without your hand cue.

Here are some words you can use:

blanket, blanke, /t/   car, ca, /r/

president, presiden, /t/   lamp, lam, /p/

crazy, craz, /y/   arcade, arca, /d/

software, softwa, /r/   mice, mi, /s/

handball, handba, /l/   chocolate, chocola, /t/

rental, renta, /l/   listen, liste, /n/

Lesson Four: Changing the Ending Sound

Tutor: I am going to say a word, and Wally is going to say a sound. Your job is to switch the ending sound of the word that I say with the sound that Wally says. For example, if I say *rug*, and Wally says /n/, you say *run*. Ready? I say *bone*.

Wally: /t/

Child: *boat*

(Notice that the spellings for the vowel sounds are different. However, the sounds are not.)

Your student may say *tone* at first, instead of *boat*. This shows he or she needs continued practice with ending sounds. Here are some words that you can use for this lesson:

lane, /s/, lace	five, /r/, fire
cheek, /r/, cheer	heart, /d/, hard
dip, /m/, dim	hat, /m/, ham
cream, /p/, creep	bike, /t/, bite
thing, /k/, think	so, /ay/, say
slow, /p/, slope	quit, /k/, quick
mood, /n/, moon	kid, /s/, kiss
grow, /ay/, gray	knob, /t/, knot

Lesson Five: Beginning or Ending Sound?

Tutor: I am going to say a word. Wally is going to say a sound. Your job is to tell me if the sound is at the beginning or the end of the word. I say *stop*. Wally says /p/. I say *end*, because the sound is at the end of the word. Ready? I say *catnip*.

Tutor: catnip

Wally: /c/

Child: *Beginning*

Here are some words and sounds you can use for this lesson:

starfish, /sh/	arrow, /ow/
butter, /b/	balance, /s/
necklace, /n/	motor, /r/
lighthouse, /l/	through, /th/
forever, /f/	hopeful, /h/
computer, /c/	money, /y/
mistake, /k/	watch, /ch/
born, /b/	social, /s/

Sometimes the words you use during the phonemic awareness activities will be ones that your student does not know. After you finish the lesson, do a quick check. For example, you might ask, "Do you know what *hopeful* means?" You don't have to ask about every word, but if you find that your student does not know a lot of words, then write in your journal the need for vocabulary development.

Lesson Six: Distinguishing Medial Sounds

Tutor: I am going to say a word. You repeat the word. If the word has the long *a* sound in it, I want you to give me a thumbs up. If it doesn't, give me a thumbs down. A long *a* sounds like the *a* in *play*. Ready? *Bean*.

Child: *Bean* (Makes a thumbs down motion.)

Tutor: *Station*

Child: *Station* (Makes a thumbs up motion.)

You can make lots of word lists for this game, using long *e* words, long *i* words, or whatever words your student needs to practice. Here is a list of words that focus on the long *a* sound:

starch (thumbs down)	navy (up)
ate (up)	Sam (down)
wave (up)	badge (down)
cane (up)	brave (up)
day (up)	Dad (down)
grape (up)	rain (up)
challenge (down)	straight (up)
lap (down)	maybe (up)
stake (up)	ape (up)

Lesson Seven: Changing the Medial Sound

Tutor: I am going to say a word, and Wally is going to say a sound. I want you to replace the medial sound of the word, or sound in the middle, with the sound Wally says. For example, if I say *pit*, and Wally says /a/, then you say *pat*. Ready? *List*.

Wally: /o/

Child: *Lost*

Here is a list of words and sounds that you can use for this lesson:

pack, /e/, peck	rug, /a/, rag
hit, /o/, hot	fox, /i/, fix
truck, /i/, trick	bad, /e/, bed
drip, /o/, drop	ship, /o/, shop
Chuck, /e/, check	mess, /i/, miss
mud, /a/, mad	glade, /i/, glide

These lessons are to get you started. It is most helpful to make a list of words in preparation for your lesson. Remember, as you do the lessons, take anecdotal notes on your student's successes and the places where he or she has difficulty. Is your student great at beginning sounds but struggling with medial sounds? If so, it's time to make more word lists focusing on medial sounds. As long as you use a puppet (and give the puppet a different voice than yours), your student should stay interested and focused during these phonemic awareness lessons. Also, don't forget to take a jump rope break!

Use humor as a teaching tool.

Teaching Strategies for Your Tutor Sessions

In the following pages we will look at several strategies for your tutoring sessions. These include:

- getting a student interested in reading

- making connections

- selecting appropriate reading materials

- reviewing and previewing

- reading to your student and helping the student develop listening skills

- oral reading

- strategies to help the beginning reader

- silent reading

- retelling

Capture Your Student's Interest in Reading

An important part of helping your student be a good reader is to select reading material that interests him or her. Use the *Interest Inventory* on page 11 to review what your student likes to read about. Ask him or her what is currently being studied in school that is of interest. Also, find out what your student wants to learn about. If you read a book that teaches facts that the child wants to learn or has personal relevance, he or she will be eager to read. Approach reading a book as if you were opening a treasure chest filled with jewels. Admire the cover, discuss the title, wonder aloud what could be inside. Then open it slowly, anticipating the beginning words. Approach reading with the intent of discovery. Discuss with your student why you should read the book.

Example:

Tutor: Ben, remember when you told me your favorite food is chocolate chip cookies? I found a book about a boy who loves chocolate just like you do. But guess what? He loves it so much he gets chocolate fever! Do you think you would ever get chocolate fever? I'm not even sure what it is.

Ben: I'll bet chocolate fever is like the flu or something. Maybe the boy gets sick because he eats too much chocolate, just like when I got sick because I ate too much watermelon.

Tutor: Maybe it is. Or maybe he burns up with fever and melts all his chocolate bars. How could we find out what chocolate fever is?

Ben: We could read the book.

Tutor: Sounds like a plan! *Chocolate Fever* by Robert K. Smith (Dell, 1978).

Make a Connection

In the above sample conversation the tutor grabbed the child's interest and set a purpose for reading. The child will want to read or listen intently to discover just what chocolate fever is. What is important, as well, is that the child has already made a personal connection with the story—he got sick from eating too much watermelon. He is predicting what could happen in this story based on his own experience. He will be eager to find out if his prediction is true.

Making connections with stories is very important if children are to remember them and take them into their hearts. When a child says "That reminds me of . . ." or "I would never do that because once I . . ." or "The boy in this story acts just like my little brother," the child is tying himself or herself to the text.

If you are reading a book about a snowman, you could ask questions such as:

- Have you ever made a snowman?
- Do you like to play in the snow?
- What time of the year does it snow?
- What do you like to do in the winter?
- What are some of the things that happen in wintertime?

Approach reading a book as if you were opening a treasure chest filled with jewels.

It is important, too, for children to make connections between one story and another. If the tutor in the above scenario wanted to promote making connections between texts, he or she could read *Charlie and the Chocolate Factory* by Roald Dahl (Puffin, 1998). You can also make connections by relating to the story yourself: "Oh, my goodness! I remember wanting to drink from a river of chocolate. Actually, I still do!"

Selecting Books

Select some books that the child has already read and enjoyed. You can even offer stories that the child is familiar with from storytelling or movies. Consider well-known fairy tales, such as *Cinderella* or *Snow White,* that are told often or have appeared on film. Repetition is very helpful in reading. As emergent readers (those just beginning to learn to read), children often choose to read the same book over and over. It is comfortable and familiar. Familiarity enables a child to fill in the gap when he or she doesn't know a word, and rereading enhances comprehension. You can reinforce this strategy by offering several books on the same theme.

When introducing a new book to a child, predictability is a plus. Predictable books that incorporate rhyme, repetition, common story structure, and/or predictable outcomes offer important clues to the reader. They help a child to successfully guess what makes sense in context or what works with the rhythm. Classic examples of such books are *Green Eggs and Ham* by Dr. Seuss (Random House, 1960) and *If You Give a Mouse a Cookie* by Laura Numeroff (Harper, 1985).

Illustrations in books can delight the reader, capture his or her attention, and guide him or her through the text. Illustrations can give important clues as well. Also remember that humor is a great learning tool as well as motivator. Joke books, riddles, silly stories, humorous poems, and even wacky tongue twisters can entice a reader.

Reviewing and Previewing Books Ahead of Time

Before you offer a book to your student, read it through and note any pertinent information that he or she should have, such as the meaning or pronunciation of new phrases, slang, foreign words, locations, or purpose for objects that may be unfamiliar. Look for appropriate places to ask questions. Be ready for your student to ask questions of you. Do not use your prepared questions if you decide not to interrupt the flow during the actual reading, but look for those "teachable moments," which can fall between chapters, before the next page, or when the child hesitates at certain words or ideas.

Preview new books with your student before you read. Allow him or her to spend an ample amount of time previewing the book with you in these ways:

- Read the title, look at the cover, and ask, "What do you think the book will be about?"

- Preview chapter headings or the table of contents, if there is one.

- In a nonfiction book, point out the glossary and index. Explain that they are there to aid the reader.

- Look at the illustrations together and take some time to talk about them.

- Ask the child to make predictions—think about what the book may be about, who the main character may be, what the character's problems or goals may be, and how the story may end. The student can make predictions at the beginning of the story, before each new chapter, before the climax of the story, right before the end, and anywhere else you feel is an appropriate place to stop and reflect.

Reading to Your Student

Many students at the second-grade level are better listeners than they are readers. And you may find that their listening skills need to be assessed and developed also. A young student needs to increase his or her ability to concentrate through listening; this will have a positive impact on all subject areas. Many children aren't given sufficient opportunity to develop their attention spans, and in second grade it still might be a struggle for them to learn to sit still, be quiet, and focus on what they hear. More often, children's visual abilities are engaged, whether it's through television, picture books, or the blackboard; auditory attunement is an important part of learning that should not be neglected.

Children learn from modeling. Listening to you read gives the child a model to emulate when rereading a book. Engage the child's interest by employing dramatic tone and facial expressions during reading.

As you read aloud, think aloud as well. Pause to ask yourself questions about word choice and meaning: *Why did the author use this word? Is it a clue? How does the main character feel about this new character?* Thinking aloud demonstrates a valuable strategy that becomes second nature as a reader progresses.

> **Reading can help develop a young student's attention span**.

Being read to increases vocabulary and verbal expression. It demonstrates how the rhythm and flow of fluent reading sounds. To help your student become a better listener, let him or her know what to listen for. Ask the child to pay special attention to pauses and emphasis. During your review, pick out some information for the child to listen for, such as: *What is the main character's favorite color?* or *How many people are in this character's family?* Ask questions about the context when you are finished to assess comprehension. Have the student retell the main points of the story. Together, imagine what may have happened next after the ending. To extend the experience, ask your student to draw a picture of one of the characters or to design his or her own book cover.

If possible, provide an audio tape that the child can take home with a favorite book. He or she can listen to the tape while reading along. You can tape yourself or ask the student to read aloud with you.

Oral Reading

When your student reads aloud, you have the opportunity to watch how he or she solves any problems he or she encounters in the text. What does your student do when he or she reaches an unknown word, and what should you do when this happens?

The first thing to remember is not to jump in and rescue the child. Remember, you are the coach. Equate this with a football game, where the coach is on the sidelines, watching and yelling "Go!" The coach doesn't jump into the game, wrest the ball from his or her team, and run to make the touchdown himself or herself. As a tutor of reading, don't tell the child the word every time he or she stumbles. The student won't develop skills to cope if you rescue him or her each time. When a barefoot child steps on a pebble and yelps

Go, Kathy, go!

"Ouch," Mom doesn't race to his or her side and drag the child to safety. Instead, she might remark, "Well, honey, how could you avoid the problem?" The child will probably put on his or her shoes. Give your student a chance to solve the reading problem himself or herself. Only if the child has tried to read the word several times using different strategies, or if it's a word that is a proper noun or unique to the story, should you give it to him or her. Remember, if the child is stumbling over five words or more per page, however, employ the Five Finger Rule (see page 18) and find an easier book.

When a child makes an error, watch him or her. Does he or she continue reading? If the word the student missed is *mother* and he or she says *mom* and keeps on reading, the meaning of the text hasn't been lost. You could say, "Are you sure that's *mom*?" and the student will probably correct it. If the child says *matter* instead of *mother*, meaning will be lost. If the student keeps on reading without making sense, then he or she isn't comprehending. Help him or her by questioning: "Does that make sense? Can you tell me what is happening in the story so far?" The child needs to learn to reread, decode the word missed, and reread again until he or she comprehends. Always be alert to the student's "state of comprehension."

To figure out the word he or she doesn't know, the child may make a prediction as to what it could be using visual information (that means the letters of the word). The student might use the strategy of predicting what the word could be based on what makes sense in the story. He or she might look for clues in an illustration. The child might try to pronounce the word and ask himself or herself if it sounds right. He or she might ask if it looks right; that is, does his or her guess match the letters of the printed word? When the student finally reads the word correctly, he or she is self-correcting. Below are a variety of methods a reader can use to self-correct.

Strategies for the Beginning Reader

Here is a list of strategies readers can use for challenging words, phrases, or passages:

- Try to figure out a word by rereading the entire sentence.

- Try blending the letters of the word out loud.

- Use clues such as illustrations and photos.

- Make an educated guess.

- Ask yourself, *Does that sound right?*

- Ask yourself, *What word would make sense here?*

- Ask for help when needed.

- Sound out the beginning sound, the ending sound, the middle sound or the vowel sound, and then try to say the word.

- Find smaller words within the word, then guess what the word is.

- Break the word down into manageable groups of letters to sound out.

- Read ahead to get context clues, then reread a passage with a difficult word.

Your role as coach is to make sure the child knows the strategies, and to make sure he or she uses them when stuck. Your student should be aware of how he or she is learning. Teach the child to verbalize what he or she does when solving a problem, as shown below:

Tutor: What strategy did you use to figure out that word?

Student: I found a little word that I already know in this bigger word.

Tutor: Excellent. That's what good readers do.

And what strategy did you use to figure out this word?

Student: I reread it and tried to figure out what would make sense. Then I looked at the picture.

Tutor: You reread it, and then you made a prediction about what the word could be based on what you know about the story. Then you looked at the picture to see if your guess made sense. Super work. You are using your strategies.

The *Picture Clues* reproducible on page 45 will help your student study a picture to look for clues about the reading. Below are ways you can prompt your student to use reading strategies. These questions and commands will focus your student's thinking on ways to solve his or her reading problems.

Your goal is to develop a student who reads with fluency. Fluent readers read smoothly, use expression and inflection, vary their speed depending on the difficulty of the text, and read in phrases. If a student reads a sentence with divisions (/) such as the ones in the following sentence, we would not deem him or her fluent. "The man in/ the black/ hat drove a big/ car."

The student is neglecting to read as we talk; he or she is not reading in phrases. Correctly read, the sentence would be divided like this: "The man in the black hat/ drove a big car."

Fluent readers process text rapidly. They anticipate words, decode easily, solve problems quickly by using what they know, such as the structure of oral language, the rhythm and cadence of oral language, and phonics. They also use their storehouse of knowledge supplied by years of "story time" at home and school.

Prompts (What to Say When a Kid Gets Stuck!)

1. Link the word to the child's background knowledge. *You like to play baseball. What position do you like to play?*

2. Suggest a clue in the illustration. *What is the girl in the picture holding?*

3. Link the word to recent reading. *The boy in yesterday's story got one for his birthday.*

4. Use auditory cues. *Does that sound right?*

5. Suggest the reader trust his or her instincts. *What word do you think it is?*

6. Have the reader look at the word more closely. *Does what you said match the letters?*

7. Ask the reader to try to recognize another word that is similar. *What word does it look like?*

8. Have the student read it again. *Try reading that sentence one more time.*

9. Have the reader look for a smaller word that is familiar in the word. *Can you find a little word in that big word?*

10. Have the reader break the word into manageable bites. *Can you break the word into smaller pieces?*

11. Move on and return to the word later. *Let's skip that word for now. Maybe as we read on, we'll find other clues that can help us figure it out.*

12. Have the student verbalize his or her strategies after figuring out a word or phrase. *How do you know that that is correct?*

Silent Reading

When a child begins to read silently, he or she is showing you that he or she is becoming independent. It is possible to read faster silently, and the more the student practices silent reading, the more fluent he or she will become. As the child learns to read silently, he or she may occasionally stop, put a finger under a word, and say it aloud. Sounding out a word is good! You know the student is using reading strategies.

Because you can't hear him or her as a student is reading silently, you need a way to know if he or she is reading correctly or understands what's being read. The use of writing to respond to reading can help you monitor your student's progress. This "literacy cycle" of reading, then writing in response to that reading, then someone else reading the response, cements the idea that reading and writing shouldn't be separated. A child must comprehend what he or she reads in order to write well about it. If your student does not understand a text and then tries to write about it, you will discover the lack of comprehension immediately. As a tutor, zero in on the difficulty and have the child go back and reread orally. Question along the way to check for comprehension. The reproducible *At the Art Fair,* on page 46, can help you get an idea of how well your student is comprehending during silent reading, and also gives you an opportunity to see how well your student can write.

What's My Connection? For a writing activity have your student create a small book or part of a journal called *What's My Connection?* Put the title at the top of each page. Then have the student copy a sentence or sentences from a story that are meaningful to him or her–that the student has personally connected with in some way. Then have the student explain the reason he or she felt connected. Encourage the student to explain why in detail. For example: *The sentence about the dog reminded me of the time my dog was lost and I found her.*

While reading, a child may come across words that he or she can decode but cannot figure out the meaning of. The *Vocabulary List* reproducible on page 47 is a form that may be used to list vocabulary words that the student doesn't know, or is unsure of, as he or she reads. When the child comes across an unknown word, he or she jots it down, writes down the page number, and keeps on reading. If, soon after, he or she is able to figure out the word due to context clues, the child puts an asterisk (*) by it. When the child is finished reading, he or she can go back and look over the

**Teach the child skills
so he or she
can read independently.**

list. First he or she writes down the meaning of the words with the asterisk, using his or her own vocabulary. The words the child doesn't know he or she can look up in a dictionary. The child will probably need your help with dictionary skills and in choosing the appropriate definition. If there are a lot of words that the student doesn't know in a given text, the text may be too difficult—remember the Five Finger Rule (page 18). After the child has defined the words and studied them, he or she should go back and reread the text. Ask the child if it makes better sense now. If the child says yes, he or she is ready to retell the story, as described below.

Retelling

One way to judge whether your student understands what he or she has read is to have the student retell the story in his or her own words. It helps to prompt the student with questions that encourage him or her to tell the story chronologically. "Then what happened?" "What did she do next?" Asking the student to retell a story will help him or her to realize that details are important and encourage the student to pay close attention. The reproducible on page 48, *Before or After?* can help your student to concentrate on chronological order in a story.

The main idea of a story is the skeleton of the story. The main idea is the answer to these questions: *Who? Did what? When? Where?* and *Why?* When a child retells a story, the main idea should be included in that retelling. The child should be able to answer the preceding questions when you ask them. If he or she can't, go back and reread until you read the answer.

As a child retells a story, listen carefully to the vocabulary he or she uses. Has the student made the story his or her own by retelling it in his or her own words? Is he or she incorporating specific details from the story (such as the creaking of a door as the scared man opened it)? Is the child

incorporating any phrases from the story (such as "I'll huff and I'll puff and I'll blow your house down!")? This would show you that the student is comprehending and retaining what is read. If necessary, begin with guided retelling. Have your student respond to questions such as:

- Where does the story take place?

- When does it take place?

- Who is the story about?

- Who else is in it?

- What is the main character's goal or problem?

- What happened?

- How did it end?

A retelling offers the student a chance to show the degree to which he can sequence the events in the story. As a tutor, you can check for understanding by observing whether or not the sequence is in order. If a child is retelling something out of order, he or she probably didn't get the gist of the story. After the student retells a story successfully, have him or her write the answers to the questions above.

Asking main idea questions should just be a skeleton of your repertoire of questioning. You need to flesh out the questions you ask, to encourage responses that demonstrate the personal connections a child makes with the story. Ask "Why?" "What do you think?" "What would you have done?" "Do you agree with that?" and so on. Again, have a conversation about the story.

Discuss feelings, express what you and your student are wondering, share different and similar points of view that the story elicits in you both. Give your personal reaction to the story and elicit your student's personal reaction to let him or her know that his or her opinion counts. Experience the power of literature by allowing yourselves to be amazed that black, squiggly lines on paper can transform the way you feel!

The student's opinion of a book is important.

More on Recordkeeping

Recordkeeping is very important as you observe a child reading. Not only do you make notes of what the child is doing, you also make notes of what you should do next. Use the recording sheet on page 49, *Record of Reading Behaviors,* as a running checklist for each book read. As you observe your student using the listed behaviors, jot down the dates. Write the name of the text he or she is reading at the top of each column. After six or so different readings, your student can reread one of the earlier texts. Compare the two readings and the strategies used. Note which strategies the child uses frequently and which ones are neglected. Focus your teaching on the neglected strategies.

Syllable Stumper

Read each word. Circle the one-syllable words in red. Circle the two-syllable words in yellow. Circle the three-syllable words in green.

brave	table	
able	difficult	
little	hillside	
adult	adventure	but
friendly	looking	middle
head	easy	hard
telephone	important	computer
glass	tissue	book
after	microphone	picture
ball	desk	apple

Picture Clues

Look at the picture below. Then circle the correct answer to each question based on the picture. Color the picture when you are finished.

1 Where is everyone playing?

in the street   in the park   in school

2 What is Sam doing under the tree?

playing ball   listening to a radio   reading

3 What is Juan feeding the squirrel?

apples   peanuts   carrots

4 What kind of day is it?

warm   cold   rainy

5 How does everyone feel?

sad   scared   happy

6 What is Jenny throwing to Jason?

football   frisbee   baseball

FS122121 The Tutor's Handbook: Reading Grade 2

At the Art Fair

Read what happened to Maria and Thomas at the school art fair. Then answer the questions.

Today is a big day for Maria and Thomas. It's the school art fair. They are helping at the third-grade booth. Everyone in their class worked hard on their art projects. Maria painted two beautiful pictures. Thomas made a sailboat out of wood. Their friend Anna made a necklace from seashells. Late in the afternoon, Maria and Thomas will visit the other booths at the fair. They can't wait to see what else is for sale.

1 Why is this a big day for Maria and Thomas?

_____

2 What are Maria and Thomas doing at the fair?

_____

3 What did Thomas make?

_____

4 What did Anna make?

_____

5 What will Maria and Thomas do later in the day?

_____

What else do you think Maria and Thomas might see at the art fair? On another sheet of paper, write about the rest of Maria's and Thomas's day at the art fair.

Vocabulary List

As you read your story, write down words whose meanings you don't know, and the page number. As you read on, if you discover what the word means, put an asterisk (*) by it. When you finish your reading, go back and explain in your own words what the "starred words" mean. Use a dictionary to help you find the meanings of the other words, and write them down. Reread the story after you know what the words mean.

_____
(Name of the story)

These are the words I don't know:	Page #	Meanings of the words:

Before or After?

Read each story. Then answer the questions by writing **B** for **before** or **A** for **after** on the lines.

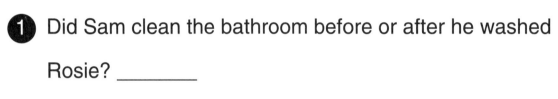

Sam washed his dog Rosie today. First he bought special soap at the pet store. Then he put Rosie in the bathtub. He turned on the water and washed Rosie. After the bath, Sam dried Rosie with a big towel. Finally, he cleaned the bathroom. Now Rosie is clean and happy.

1 Did Sam clean the bathroom before or after he washed

Rosie? _____

2 Did Sam buy special soap before or after he put Rosie in the

bathtub? _____

3 Did Sam dry Rosie before or after he turned on the water? _____

Tina's class visited the space museum. The teacher bought tickets. Then she gave each child a map of the museum. Next, the class visited a room with pictures of spaceships. Afterward, the children learned more about space travel. Then they ate lunch. When they returned to school, each child wrote a story about the museum.

4 Did the teacher buy tickets before or after she gave out maps?

_____

5 Did the class eat lunch before or after they learned about space

travel? _____

5 Did the children write a story before or after they visited the

space museum? _____

Name _____

Record of Reading Behaviors

Reading Behavior   **Name of Text**

1 Previews book					
2 Makes predictions					
3 Finds smaller words within a word					
4 Blends letters out loud					
5 Rereads to self-correct					
6 Uses illustrations as clues					
7 Makes educated guesses					
8 Reads ahead to find context clues					
9 Uses phonics					
10 Reads with expression					
11 Reads punctuation with inflection					
12 Reads with fluency					
13 Reads in phrases					
14 Makes connections to self					
15 Makes connections to other texts					
16 Enjoys reading					
17 Other					

SAMPLE TUTORIAL LESSON

This chapter offers a sample one-hour lesson plan. It contains listening activities, oral reading activities, and silent reading activities. Included are suggested lengths of time for each activity. Experiment with the guidelines to best fulfill your student's needs. As a tutor, you have the freedom to tailor the tutoring session according to what your student's individual requirements are.

A Sample Lesson

Tutor Reads to Student (15 minutes)

Tutor: Ben, this is a new story called *Superhero Sam*. I chose this book because I know that you like superheroes. What do you like about superheroes?

Ben: I like that they're so strong.

Tutor: Let's skim through the book and take a look at the pictures. What do you notice?

(Ben skims through the pages. He reads some words, touches some pictures.)

Ben: I notice that Superhero Sam does not look very strong. In fact, his arms look really wimpy.

Tutor: What do you think this story will be about?

Ben: Well, if he's a superhero and he's wimpy, maybe he's a bad superhero.

Tutor: That prediction makes sense! Let's see if you're right. Look at the book with me and listen while I read.

Superhero Sam
by Sally Cardoza Griffin

Tutor: (begins to read) *Superhero Sam walked down the street licking a chocolate ice-cream cone. His trainer had told him he needed more protein, but Superhero Sam just loved ice cream. It was his one weakness.*

Ben: (interrupts) What does that mean?

Tutor: A weakness is something he has a hard time saying no to.

Ben: Oh! I have a weakness for playing video games.

Tutor: You and Superhero Sam have made a connection then!

Tutor: (continues story) *As he licked his ice-cream cone, Superhero Sam pondered how to solve the mayor's big problem. The mayor of Sundown City was very mad about all the robberies taking place. A gang of thieves was breaking into all the bakeries in town and stealing, not money, but baked goods—pastries, pies, cookies, and cakes!*

Now, Mayor Tuttle was a man who enjoyed his breakfast bear claw. He had not had one in weeks.

Ben: (interrupts) Um, wait. He eats bear claws?

Tutor: A bear claw is a pastry with nuts and cinnamon. The baker shapes it like the paw of a bear. They're my dad's favorite pastry. Would you like me to bring you one next week?

Ben: Sure!

Tutor: (continues the story) *"Sam," the mayor thundered, "find those thieves. I miss my bear claws. I miss my angel food cake. I must have those villains in handcuffs before sundown!*

Superhero Sam finished his ice-cream cone and wiped his hands on a napkin. He threw it in the handy waste can outside All Cities' Gym. Then he went inside to lift weights. Superhero Sam was rather skinny. He had only enough muscle to hold up his bones and his head. The people of Sundown City wanted a superhero who looked like Superman or Spiderman. But Sam was only medium-sized, with black glasses and a buzz cut, though he had a very nice smile. Trying his hardest to fit the image of a superhero, Sam worked out every day. He did bench presses and arm curls. He did sit-ups and push-ups. He ran on the treadmill and stair machine. All the time he worked out, he thought about how to catch the pastry thieves.

The other superheroes at the gym offered him advice. "You need a race car that can get you to the scene of the crime fast. That way, you could catch the thieves as they try to get away," said one hero. Another said, "You should learn how to throw nets like I do, and tie them up as fast as I can say 'arachnid.'"

"They'd never escape from me," said another, as he flexed his biceps. "I could hold them with one hand tied behind my back."

Superhero Sam thanked the superheroes for their suggestions. He appreciated their help, but he had a mind of his own. He knew that the thieves got away with the last haul yesterday. They stole a dozen birthday cakes made for all the birthday boys and girls of Sundown City. And that had gotten him thinking. He showered, changed into his khaki pants and short sleeved button-down, laced up his walking shoes, and walked back to the ice-cream store. While he waited for his double-scooped, fudge and caramel, peanut butter bomb cone, he made a phone call. Then he sat back in a lavender chair and enjoyed his treat.

Suddenly, three men dressed in white suits came banging through the door. One shouted, "This is a robbery! Give us all your ice cream!"

The clerk glanced wide-eyed at Sam. Sam gave her a nice smile. Outside there was a

screech of cars and wailing sirens. Sam quietly got up and opened the door. A dozen police officers swarmed the three white-suited men. The officers handcuffed the thieves and took them to jail.

The next day, Mayor Tuttle shook Sam's hand at the Superhero Award Assembly. "How did you know where they'd strike next, Sam? These were pastry robbers. I thought you'd stake out Freddy's Fresh and Tasty Bakery next."

Superhero Sam smiled slyly. "Well, all I had to do was a little thinking. After all, what goes better with cake than ice cream?"

The End

Phonemic Awareness Work (15 minutes)

Tutor: Well, Ben, what did you think of that story?

Ben: I really liked it. I never knew a superhero didn't need muscles.

Tutor: Did your prediction come true? That he wouldn't be good because he was a wimp?

Ben: No, it didn't come true. Sam was really good. He got the robbers. But how did the police know to come to the ice-cream store?

Tutor: What did Sam do while he waited for his ice-cream cone?

Ben: I don't remember. Let's reread.

Tutor: *While he waited for his double-scooped, fudge and caramel, peanut butter bomb cone, he made a phone call.*

Ben: He called 911!

Tutor: He called the police, didn't he? What did Sam use instead of muscles?

Ben: He used his brain!

Tutor: Right! Now it's time to get up and stretch. Let's toss the beanbag. I've got a new word game to teach you.

As they toss the beanbag, they chant: "Hey, hey, don't be late. Come in through the garden gate! What did you bring us for the feast? What did you bring that's good to eat? What did you bring that starts with *A?*" Toss the beanbag back and forth, each saying an *A* word (*apple, alligator, apricot, astronaut*); then move on to *B*, and so on.

Tutor: Okay, Ben, good work. Do you remember that last week you had difficulty remembering the sound */aw/?* Let's play a word-ending game with Wally. (Tutor puts puppet on his or her hand.) You are going to make words that end with the sound */aw/.* Wally is going to say a beginning sound. I want you to put the sound that Wally says on the beginning of the sound */aw/* to make a new word. Here we go.

Wally: */l/*

Ben: *Law*

Wally: */s/*

Ben: *Saw*

Wally: */cl/*

Ben: *Claw.* Like bear claw!

Tutor: Good connection!

Wally continues with */dr/, /c/, /p/, /str/,* and so on.

Tutor: Now I'm going to say some words with the sound */aw/* and some words without that sound. I want you to give me a thumbs-up signal if you hear the sound /aw/ anywhere in the word. Give me a thumbs-down if you don't hear the sound. Here we go. *Awful* (thumbs-up). *Crawl* (thumbs-up). *Spoil* (thumbs-down). *Alex* (thumbs-down). *Everyone* (thumbs-down). *Strawberry* (thumbs-up).

Tutor: Next I want you to listen to the sound /ou/. If I say a word that has /ou/ in it, put your hands on your head. If I say a word with /aw/ in it, put your hands on your knees. *Pounce* (head). *Awesome* (knees). *Out* (head). *Bound* (head). *Raw* (knees). *Ouch!* (head). *Flaw* (knees). Terrific, Ben. The next story we read will have some words with the /ou/ sound in them.

Student Reads Aloud to Tutor (15 minutes)

Tutor: Okay, Ben, it's time for you to practice your reading strategies. Can you tell me something a good reader does when he is stuck?

Ben: Reread. Or look at the hard word and try to find a little word in it that he knows.

Tutor: Exactly right. Let's write that on your *What Do Good Readers Do?* chart. Can you write those strategies down for me? Excellent. Now, let's take a look at our book. This is a book about a mouse. She's a very unhappy mouse. Take a "walk" through the pictures and see what you can learn about the mouse.

Ben: (Looks at pictures.) The mouse isn't eating cheese. She's eating something else, but I don't know what it is. Oh, no! She's eating cat food. Look, she's trying to make her ears go pointy.

Tutor: How do you know it's a girl mouse?

Ben: 'Cause she has a bow on her head, and her name is Mabel. (pronounces it with a short *a* sound)

Tutor: *Ma bel?* I've never heard that name. What else could it be?

Ben: I see *abe* like in *Abe Lincoln*. Oh, it's *Mabel*.

Tutor: Yes, that's right. What's she gluing on her tail?

Ben: She's gluing those white things on that we used to make Santa's beards in my classroom.

Tutor: She's gluing cotton balls on her tail. Why do you think she would do that?

Ben: Maybe she wants to be a cat?

Tutor: Why don't you read to find out? I'm going to be jotting down notes to myself as you read. Don't worry about what I write down. You just worry about reading. And remember, you're going to read some words with that /ou/ sound.

Ben reads the following story out loud.

Mabel the Mouse
by Sally Cardoza Griffth

Ben: *Mabel the Mouse needed a change. She was tired of being gray. She was tired of being small. She was tired of eating cheese. She was tired of her round ears. She was especially tired of her long, skinny tail. Mabel was tired of being a mouse!* (Ben said *tried* instead of *tired*. Ben self-corrects and rereads the sentences. Tutor notes *self-correction due to meaning*.)

Ben: *She spent all day peeking out of her mouse hole in the kitchen. She watched Rosie the Cat as she licked her calico fur.*

What does *calico* mean?

Tutor: *Calico* means a cat with three colors of fur.

Ben: (continues reading): *Mabel watched Rosie the Cat jump up on the table as if it were no higher than a footstool. She watched Rosie eat her crunchy dry cat food, then clean her pointy ears and long, fluffy tail. "That's it!" Mabel cried. "I'm becoming a cat. They are not boring, like me."*

Mabel the Mouse waited till Rosie the Cat was asleep. She crept out of her hole and squeezed into a canister marked Flour. She'd seen the lady of the house use this white powder lots of times. "Aachoo!" she sneezed, and froze. Had Rosie heard her? "Whew," she thought, when no cat pounced.

Hey! Here is an /ou/ word! Pounced.

Mabel looked at herself. "Look at me. I'm so white and lovely, not a boring gray color. But my goodness, this powder makes me sneezy."

Next, Mabel tried to jump onto the table like Rosie had done. She held herself as tall as she could and sprang up, and "OUCH!"

Hey, there's another one! (Tutor notes Ben is recognizing /ou/ words.)

Mabel crashed into the table leg! She froze. Had Rosie heard her? Whew! she thought, when no cat pounced. Next Mabel limped over to the cat food bowl. Curious, she took a little nibble of the crunchy, dry food. Crunch, crunch, crunch. Yuck, thought Mabel. This tastes like fish dust! She wished she had some cheese to get that nasty taste out of her mouth. But, she thought, cheese is so boring.

Next, Mabel sneaked into the bathroom. She took some hair gel from a bottle that the boy of the house used to make his hair all pointy.

My brother uses blue hair gel. (Tutor notes that Ben made a connection.)

Mabel rubbed it all over her two round ears, and tried to make them pointy. But all she got were two sticky round ears. "Well," she murmured, "at least they smell nice." Then she crept into a bag of cotton balls that was on the sink and grabbed some. (Ben pronounces grabbed as two syllables.

Tutor: "Does that sound right?" Ben can't read the word, so the tutor says, "It's one syllable. Don't break it up." (Tutor notes that they need to work on more one-syllable past tense words.)

Ben: (continues to read) *Mabel then hurried out to a desk where the girl of the house kept her glue. Mabel dipped her tail in the glue and started sticking the cotton balls on her tail. "Lovely," she exclaimed, as she admired her tail. But then Mabel sneezed again. She froze. Had Rosie heard her?*

"Meow," snarled Rosie, and pounced at Mabel. (Ben says "snareled." Tutor tells him the word, then notes that she needs to work with /ar/ words.)

Ben: (continues to read) *Mabel tried to run fast, but her tail full of cotton was slowing her down. Her sticky ears were dripping on the carpet. The flour was making her nose run. The dry, crunchy cat food wasn't sitting so well in her stomach, and her leg hurt! "Oh, please, oh, please, let me reach my safe, boring hole in the wall!" Mabel cried.*

As quickly as possible, Mabel scurried into her safe hole. The first thing she did—after taking a bath and washing off all the flour and gel and pulling off all the cotton—was to nibble a nice piece of tasty cheese.

The End

Ben: That was a good story. I guess she would rather be bored than be a cat.

Tutor: Did your prediction come true, Ben?

Ben: Yes.

Tutor: What strategies did you use when you figured out that the word was *tired* instead of *tried?*

Ben: Well, when I said "Mabel was tried of being a mouse," it didn't make sense. So, I reread it and put my finger under the word. Then I read it "tired," and it made sense.

Tutor: What happened at the word *snarled?*

Ben: I didn't know it.

Tutor: What strategy could you have used?

Ben: I guess I could have put another word there, like *growled.* But it didn't match.

Tutor: It would have made sense, but you're right about it not matching. Ben, remember the sound /ar/? We're going to work on that more. Now, can you tell me what connections you made to the story?

Ben: My brother uses hair gel too. He gets the counter all sticky and my mom tells him to clean it. I have a cat, but it's not a calico. It's all black. I wish I had a mouse for a pet. Do you think a mouse could really stick cotton balls on its tail?

Tutor: I don't think it would be too nice for a mouse if we tried to find out! You made lots of connections between yourself and the story. Did the story remind you of any other story?

Ben: My teacher read *The Little Rabbit Who Wanted Red Wings.* That rabbit didn't like being a rabbit and grew red wings so he could fly. Boy, did he have problems. In the end, he went back to normal, just like Mabel. (Tutor notes that Ben is making connections.)

Tutor: Why do you suppose they went back to normal?

Ben: I guess it was easier just to be themselves.

Tutor: Ben, could you draw three pictures that would tell the story we just read? What would you draw for the beginning, the middle, and the end? I'm going to fold this paper into three parts. I want you to take your marker and draw the three pictures.

Ben: Okay. First I'd draw Mabel looking out of her mouse hole. She'd have a sad face on. I'd draw one of those bubble things over her head. It says *I wish I were a cat!* For the middle I'd have to draw her getting into all the things. I guess I'd just draw her with the hair gel on her ears and cotton on her tail. And at the end I'd draw her in the bathtub with a smile on her face. I'd put the cat looking in her mouse hole, though.

Tutor: Could you use those drawings to help you retell the story?

Ben: Yes, I guess, but I left a lot out. I could just say the words, though.

Tutor: You mean your drawings sort of give you a hint, and then your brain fills in all the other parts when you're retelling the story out loud.

Ben: Yes.

Tutor: Good. Next week I want you to use those pictures to help you retell the story of Mabel. Now it's time for you to read to yourself and answer my questions about this poem. Use a new vocabulary list to jot down any words you don't know. Remember the reading strategies we learned.

Silent Reading (15 minutes)

Ben reads almost silently. He moves his lips a little bit. The tutor is ready to support him; she watches his eyes to see if he lingers on a certain passage, to see if he's checking pictures, to see if he's rereading. She watches the words he writes on his vocabulary sheet. If there are too many, she questions him to determine if the text is too hard.

The Hawk in the House
by Sally Cardoza Griffith

"Run for your lives!" shrieked Mother Mouse;
"Find a safe place to hide, there's a hawk in the house!"
"Who left the door open?" we heard Father shout,
While Mother was yelling, "Get that hawk out!"
My sister and I cowered under our beds,
As that hawk swooped and glided over our heads.
Mother scurried quickly across the vast floor,
While Father was grumbling, "Who opened that door?"

Huddled together, the four of us clung;
We whispered our prayers, thought of songs we had sung.
Our parents kept saying, "We'll all be just fine."
I had trouble believing that one little line.
'Cause that hawk kept on flying, around and around,
And he kept on making that scary hawk sound.
I had to do something, I had to act fast;
I didn't know how much longer we'd last!

I looked around quickly and came up with a plan;
I snatched my toy lizard, which I tied to my hand.
I flung it across to the wide open door,
And wriggled the string so Liz "crawled" on the floor.

The hawk took one look and snatched it up in her beak;
As I untied my hand, I heard my mom squeak,
"Oh, it flew out the door, that huge hawk is gone!
I'm ever so thankful that no harm's been done."
We all closed our eyes, and each said our thanks,
And then my father started nailing up planks.
"This door will stay closed, we'll use that small crack;
It's much better than being a hawk's midday snack."
I quite agreed and helped nail up the wood;
I didn't want that door open, not when I could
Forget once to close it, like earlier today,
And if Dad asks who did it, oh, what should I say?

The End

Tutor: Ben, now that you're finished, I'd like you to tell me what happened in this poem.

Ben: A hawk got into some mice's house and they all had to hide.

Tutor: And then what happened?

Ben: Well, there was this one mouse, not the mother or father or sister, but the boy mouse.

Tutor: Did he have a name?

Ben: No. Anyway the boy mouse ties a toy lizard to a string and the hawk gets it and flies away.

Tutor: And then what happened?

Ben: The mice said thanks and then the dad nailed the door shut.

Tutor: Who left the door open?

Ben: I'm not sure. I need to reread. . . . Yes, the mouse with no name left it open. Is he going to tell his dad he left it open?

Tutor: What do you think? What would you do?

The tutor ends the session by having Ben write a retelling of the poem. She reviews the *Vocabulary List* reproducible (page 47) Ben is completing for the poem and checks to see if Ben put an asterisk by any of the words. For the time remaining, Ben writes definitions of the vocabulary words with the tutor's support. Then the tutor gives Ben a bookmark (page 13) to fill in. Ben's homework is to practice reading the poem and to finish his vocabulary list. The tutor and Ben give each other a high-five for a job well done.

RECOMMENDED READING MATERIALS FOR SECOND GRADERS

Fiction Picture Books

Aardema, Verna. *Bringing the Rain to Kapiti Plain.* Dial Books, 1981.
This is the rhyming story of a boy named Ki-pat who saved the plain of Kapiti from a terrible drought.

————. *Why Mosquitoes Buzz in People's Ears:* A West African Tale. Dial Books, 1975.

Iguana gets so irritated by mosquito's tales that he puts sticks in his ears. Because he can't hear due to the sticks in his ears, a series of misunderstandings ensues, causing panic and thus disaster in the jungle. The animals hold court and determine, finally, that the mosquito is to blame.

Allard, Harry. *Miss Nelson Is Missing.* Houghton Mifflin, 1977.
What happened to Miss Nelson, the kind and beautiful teacher who had a disobedient class? And who is this wicked-looking substitute teacher Miss Viola Swamp, who makes the disobedient children work without stopping? Will Miss Nelson ever return?

Bailey, Carolyn Sherwin. *The Little Rabbit Who Wanted Red Wings.* Price Stern Sloan, 1988.
A little rabbit wishes to be different; he wishes for red wings like a bird. His wish comes true, but he is very disappointed by the fact that no one recognizes him and he can't fly. A poignant tale that teaches one to be careful for what one wishes!

Barrett, Judi. *Cloudy with a Chance of Meatballs.* Atheneum, 1982.
Look at the sky. Is it a bird? Is it a plane? No, it's meatballs! In the land of Chewandswallow, food falls from the sky to provide nourishment for the people. But something goes haywire, and the meatballs are the size of basketballs. What will the people of Chewandswallow do?

Brett, Jan. *The Mitten: A Ukrainian Folktale.* Putnam, 1989.
This is a beautifully illustrated story of how a little boy's lost mitten becomes the home to many forest animals.

Brown, Marcia. *Stone Soup.* Scribners, 1947.
How do you feed hungry soldiers with soup made from a stone? Villagers are tricked into cooking a tasty dish for these clever men.

Burton, Virginia. *The Little House.* Houghton Mifflin, 1978.
A little house in the country that was once well-loved is abandoned as the big city grows all around her. This story shows the drama of urbanization and how the passage of time affects a town. The little house is eventually rescued and moved to the country once again.

Cooney, Barbara. *Miss Rumphius.* Viking, 1982.
A grandfather wishes for his granddaughter to make the world more beautiful; and so begins the journey of Miss Rumphius. From childhood to old age she searches for a way to fulfill her grandfather's wish. Finally, she spreads flower seeds across the land of the village by the sea, and soon, beauty blooms everywhere.

DePaola, Tomie. *The Legend of the Bluebonnet.* Putnam, 1996.
Lovely blue flowers, the bluebonnets, cover the state of Texas. This story explains how they came to bloom. A young Comanche Indian girl loses her family in a terrible drought. Someone from her village must offer a sacrifice to the spirits in order to end the drought. The little girl sacrifices her beloved doll, and the flowers bloom as the drought ends.

———. *Strega Nona: Her Story.* Prentice Hall, 1975.
Oh, no! Big Anthony uses magic to start the spaghetti cooking, but doesn't know how to stop the magic. What will Big Anthony do?

The Fisherman and His Wife. Retold by John Warren Stewig. Holiday, 1988.
A fisherman catches a magic fish who grants wishes to the fisherman and his wife. The wife becomes increasingly greedy, demanding more and more wishes, so the fish teaches the two a lesson about gratitude.

Flack, Marjorie. *Ask Mister Bear.* Macmillan, 1932, 1958, 1960.
With the help of Mister Bear, a little boy decides what to give his mother for her birthday.

Freeman, Don. *Corduroy.* Viking, 1968.
Realizing that he does not look new, a little stuffed bear searches through a department store for his lost button, so that someone will buy him and give him a home. He does not find his button, but a little girl buys him anyway, showing Corduroy the meaning of friendship and unconditional love.

Gag, Wanda. *Millions of Cats.* Putnam, 1996.
An old lonely man searches for a kitty to be company for himself and his wife. He can't decide which kitten he likes the best, so he takes home millions of cats. The cats have an interesting way of solving the problem of which cat gets to live there.

Galdone, Paul. *The Little Red Hen.* Clarion, 1973.
This is the story of a little hen who does all the work while her friends laze about. She alone enjoys the fruits of her labors, teaching the lesson that if you want something, you must work for it.

Hall, Donald. *Ox-Cart Man.* Viking, 1979.
This lovely cycle story shows how life in early New England revolved around raising crops and animals and making such things as shawls, mittens, and birch brooms to be sold in Portsmouth Market. The money earned would be used to buy seeds, feed for the animals, and other items in order to begin again.

Hoban, Russell. *Bread and Jam for Frances.* Harper, 1964.
All Frances wants to eat is bread and jam, for breakfast, lunch, and dinner. Her mother, a wise woman, lets her. As her family feasts on spaghetti dinners and egg breakfasts, Frances chews her bread and jam, but less and less enthusiastically. Finally, she can take it no more, and her mother packs her a lovely lobster salad for lunch.

Hutchins, Pat. *The Doorbell Rang.* Houghton, 1989.

Children try to share cookies that their mom baked, but each time the cookies are divided, more friends come to the house. Just when the children think there will not be enough to share, Grandma arrives with a freshly baked batch of cookies.

Kraus, Robert. *Leo the Late Bloomer.* Illustrated by Jose Aruego and Ariane Aruego. Croswell, 1971.

Leo is a young tiger whose father worries about his inability to talk, read, and write. Leo's mother reassures his father that Leo is simply a "late bloomer." Children who identify with Leo will be comforted and encouraged by this charming story.

Lester, Helen. *Tacky the Penguin.* Houghton Mifflin, 1988.

Tacky the Penguin marches to the beat of his own drummer, and his other penguin pals get annoyed. Yet Tacky manages to save the day in his own very wacky way.

Lionni, Leo. *Alexander and the Wind-up Mouse.* Pantheon, 1969.

Alexander is a real mouse. He becomes good friends with a wind-up mouse named Willy and wants to be just like him. Then Alexander discovers Willy is to be thrown away. Alexander must discover a way to help his friend before it's too late.

———. *Frederick.* Pantheon, 1967.

Frederick is a little gray mouse who, while his family is getting ready for winter by storing food, gathers memories of the beautiful summer and autumn days. During the dismal gloom of winter, Frederick shares what he's gathered: lovely phrases that express the beauty that he remembers. He warms the hearts of his family on the darkest days of winter.

Lobel, Arnold. *Frog and Toad Are Friends.* Harper, 1979.

This book contains five tales of two best friends. Frog and Toad have fun, argue, challenge each other, and take care of each other. The stories explore many avenues of the relationship between friends.

Louie, Ai-Ling. *Yeh Shen: A Cinderella Story from China.* Philomel, 1982.

A wicked stepmother, an evil stepsister, the young dainty girl who must suffer at their hands—this tale has it all, even a magic fish. Yeh Shen must overcome the hurdles placed in her life by her stepfamily in order to marry her prince.

McCloskey, Robert. *Blueberries for Sal.* Viking, 1948.

Sal and her mother go to pick blueberries to can for winter. Sal wanders away from her mother, just as a little bear wanders away from his mother. They each find the other's mother, and everyone is surprised as can be.

Milne, A.A. *Winnie-the-Pooh.* Dutton, 1961.

This is the famous story of Christopher Robin and his stuffed toys—Pooh, Piglet, Kanga, and Roo—and the adventures they have playing make-believe.

Mosel, Arlene. *Tikki Tikki Tembo.* Holt, 1995.

A great read aloud, this funny legend tells why the Chinese people changed from giving their first-born sons long names to giving them short ones.

Munsch, Robert. *Thomas' Snowsuit.* Annick, 1985.

Thomas does not want to wear his new snowsuit, no matter who insists! Not his mother, teacher, or even his principal can make him wear it. Children laugh aloud when reading this story.

Numeroff, Laura. *If You Give a Mouse a Cookie.* Harper, 1985.
A polite little boy gives a mouse a cookie, then the mouse wants a glass of milk, and so on, until the mouse has created a whirlwind of demands, and the polite little boy is an exhausted little boy.

Peet, Bill. *Big Bad Bruce.* Houghton, 1977.
Bruce is a big shaggy bear who scares all the other animals in the forest. He meets his match in a clever witch who shrinks him down to a size small enough that he will get a taste of his own medicine.

Penn, Audrey. *The Kissing Hand.* Scholastic, 1993.
This is a loving tale about Chester the Raccoon, who is nervous about leaving his mother for the first day of school. Mother shows him a special way to remember her; then Chester reminds her of how much he loves her.

Potter, Beatrix. *The Tale of Peter Rabbit.* Warne, 1987.
This is the story of the adventures of a naughty rabbit named Peter who, against the sage advice of his mother, dares to invade the garden of Mr. McGregor.

Reeves, James. *Fables From Aesop.* Bedrick/Blackie, 1985.
This book contains 50 fables. Children love to figure out the lesson in each one and apply it to their own lives.

Rey, H.A. *Curious George.* Houghton Mifflin, 1973.
George is a curious little monkey who, even with the man in the big yellow hat looking after him, always seems to get into mischief. There are many of these classic stories in the series.

Sendak, Maurice. *Where the Wild Things Are.* Harper, 1984.
When a little boy is sent to bed without his supper, his imagination carries him far away from his bedroom to the land of the wild things, where he is king.

Seuss, Dr. *The Cat in the Hat.* Random House, 1957.
It's a rainy day, and what will two children left alone do? They let the cat in the hat enter their house, and mischief begins. How will they ever get rid of him before their mother gets home?

———. *Green Eggs and Ham.* Random House, 1960.
The classic picture book with rhythmic, predictable verses that children find reassuring to read.

Silverstein, Shel. *The Giving Tree.* Harper, 1964.
This book is about true friendship and the sacrifice a tree makes so someone she loves can be happy.

Van Allsburg, Chris. *The Polar Express.* Houghton Mifflin, 1985.
Can you hear the silver bell ring? Journey to the North Pole with a little boy to visit Saint Nicholaus's world and discover if you still believe in Santa Claus.

Viorst, Judith. *Alexander and the Terrible, Horrible, No Good, Very Bad Day.* Atheneum, 1972.
Poor Alexander! He wakes up with gum stuck in his hair, the teacher doesn't appreciate his artwork, he has to buy plain old white sneakers, and he has lima beans for supper. What a terrible day!

Waber, Bernard. *Ira Sleeps Over.* Houghton Mifflin, 1972.
Ira can't wait to sleep over at his friend's house. But he faces a big problem. Should he take his teddy bear with him?

Williams, Margery. *The Velveteen Rabbit.* Doubleday, 1958.
A toy rabbit longs to be real, and because of the love of a little boy, the rabbit's wish becomes true.

Wood, Audrey. *The Napping House.* Harcourt, 1984.
It's a rainy day, and everyone in the house is taking a nap, from Grandma to the flea on the dog. When the bed breaks, surprise and laughter reign, and the sun begins to shine.

Yashima, Taro. *Crow Boy.* Viking, 1955.
A little boy in a village school in Japan stares at the walls, sits under the desk, and watches the ceiling, until the day his new sixth-grade teacher encourages him to pin his art on the wall, and then invites him to imitate the crows. The people are amazed to realize that this boy has incredible talents. His talents are simply different than their own.

Young, Ed. *Lon Po Po: A Red-Riding Hood Story from China.* Philomel, 1989.
Take a big bad wolf, a sick grandmother, and a mother cautioning her three daughters not to let anyone in the house, and what do you get? An intriguing Red-Riding Hood story, where the little girls themselves solve their problem.

Zion, Gene. *Harry the Dirty Dog.* Harper Junior Books, 1956.
A white dog with black spots runs away from home to avoid taking a bath. When he returns home, he is so dirty that his family does not recognize him. In order to convince the family that he is their dog, Harry dashes into the house and voluntarily jumps into the bathtub. After a good scrubbing, he is recognized and welcomed back into the family.

Poetry

Baylor, Byrd. *When Clay Sings.* Scribner, 1972.
Broken bits of pottery tell the story of the Southwestern Native Americans' way of life in earlier times. Read this story aloud while playing a cassette of Native American music.

Cole, Joanna. *Anna Banana: 101 Jump-Rope Rhymes.* Morrow, 1989.
Fun word play that students will love to read and recite.

de Regniers, Beatrice Schenk, et al., comps. *Sing a Song of Popcorn: Every Child's Book of Poems.* Scholastic, 1988.
Beautifully illustrated by Caldecott Award–winners, this book of poems takes the reader through the four seasons. It enchants with poems about animals and people doing everyday things.

Hoberman, Mary Ann. *A House Is a House for Me.* Viking, 1978.
"Where do you live?" is not such a basic question. "A rose is a house for a smell" and "A throat is a house for a hum" are examples of the creative thinking that is alive in this book.

Hopkins, Lee Bennett. *The Sky Is Full of Song.* Harper Junior Books, 1983.
Children will experience the moods of each season in these 38 short poems.

Kroll, Virginia. *Jaha and Jamil Went Down the Hill: An African Mother Goose.* Charlesbridge, 1995.
Diverse aspects of African life are told through new lyrics to familiar rhyme patterns.

Prelutsky, Jack. *The New Kid on the Block.* Greenwillow, 1984.
Children delight in this book of more than 100 silly, outrageous poems.

———. *The Random House Book of Poetry for Children.* Random House, 1983.
This is a wonderful anthology of 572 traditional and contemporary poems organized by themes, such as food, home, animals, goblins, and children.

Silverstein, Shel. *Where the Sidewalk Ends.* Harper, 1974.
A terrific collection of 130 poems by an author who understands children. With titles like "Bandaids" and "The Dirtiest Man in the World," how can a child resist?

Yolen, Jane, ed. *Street Rhymes Around the World.* Boyds Mills, 1972.
This book contains 17 bilingual rhymes. The rhymes are illustrated by artists from their countries of origin.

Chapter Books

Atwater, Richard, and Florence Atwater. *Mr. Popper's Penguins.* Dell, 1978.
Mr. Popper is an ordinary house painter with some extraordinary guests—12 penguins!

Baum, L. Frank. *The Wizard of Oz.* Ballantine, 1985.
This is the original, magical story of Dorothy and her friends as they journey to the Emerald City. This is but the first of 14 books on the Land of Oz by Baum.

Banks, Lynne Reid. *The Indian in the Cupboard.* Doubleday, 1981.
A nine-year-old English boy accidentally causes a toy American Indian to come to life. The boy faces the immense responsibility of caring for his new friend from another time and another culture.

Burnett, Frances Hodgson. *The Secret Garden.* Viking, 1989.

This book was first published in 1911. It is the story of a little girl who is orphaned and must live with her indifferent uncle in an English manor house. Upon exploring the grounds, she discovers a secret garden and, later, the invalid son of her uncle, who becomes her friend.

Catling, Patrick Skene. *The Chocolate Touch.* Morrow, 1979.
Everything John touches turns to chocolate, including his eggs and bacon, his trumpet, his pencils, and his toothpaste. This is another lesson in the old adage, "Be careful what you wish for!"

Cleary, Beverly. *Ramona and Her Father.* Morrow, 1977.
Ramona is in second grade, and life becomes complicated when her dad loses his job.

Cohen, Miriam. *Second Grade Friends.* Scholastic Inc., 1993.
Second graders form friendships and have fun in this beginning chapter book for young readers.

Dahl, Roald. *James and the Giant Peach.* Knopf, 1961.
James is a little boy who is orphaned. He must live with his mean aunts and act as their servant. His life changes when a bit of magic causes an ordinary peach tree to produce a giant peach, complete with a whole set of critters living inside who become James's new friends.

Martin, Ann M. *Teacher's Pet.* Scholastic Inc., 1995.
The kids in Ms. Coleman's second-grade class decide to adopt a class pet.

McCloskey, Robert. *Homer Price.* Puffin, 1976.
This is a modern classic about a boy's hilarious adventures in a small town.

Smith, Robert K. *Chocolate Fever.* Dell, 1978.
With chocolate cake for breakfast and chocolate sprinkles on his cereal, it's inevitable that Henry Green comes down with chocolate fever. Indeed, one learns in this book that moderation is the key to a healthy diet.

Nonfiction

Aliki, *My Five Senses.* Harper, 1989.
This bright and simple book teaches how we learn about the world around us through the five senses. Part of the Let's-Read-and-Find-Out-Science series.

DePaola, Tomie. *The Popcorn Book.* Holiday House, 1978.
This book is filled with fascinating and humorous facts about popcorn that kids will enjoy.

Gibbons, Gail. *Fire! Fire!* Crowell Junior Books, 1984.
Firefighters use a variety of methods to extinguish different types of fires.

Hirst, Robin, and Sally Hirst. *My Place in Space.* Orchard, 1988.
This comic tale looks at a child who knows his street address, and also his planet, galaxy, and beyond.

Kitchen, Bert. *Somewhere Today.* Candlewick Press, 1992.
The curious habits of eagles, hares, salamanders, and many other animals, taught through descriptive language and detailed paintings, will fascinate young readers.

Morris, Ann. *Houses and Homes.* Lothrop, Lee, and Shepard, 1992.
A photographic view of houses around the world. The different dwellings will invite discussion and personal connections.

Schwartz, David M. *How Much Is a Million?* Lothrop, Lee, and Shepard, 1985.
A witty, fun book that explains numbers up to one trillion.

Peters, Lisa Westberg. *The Sun, the Wind and the Rain.* Henry Holt, 1988.
A simple lesson in geology that uses a young girl's play with sand on the beach to illustrate the evolution of a mountain.

Ranger Rick. National Wildlife Federation.
This monthly periodical has articles, photographs, activities, and a Web site: www.nwf.org/rrick.

Zoehfeld, Kathleen Weidner. *What's Alive?* HarperCollins, 1995.
Science concepts are explained in simple terms in this book, part of the Let's-Read-and-Find-Out-Science series.

Zoobooks. Publisher: Kenneth Kitson. Wildlife Education, Limited.
Each issue of this magazine is devoted to a type of animal. The photographs are superb, and the information is complete and well written.